This Participant's Guide belongs to:

https://MGRush.com

All rights reserved. No part of this book may be reproduced or used in any manner without the prior written permission of the copyright owner, except for the use of brief quotations in a book review.

To request permissions, contact the publisher at
Training@MGRushFacilitation.com

Copyright © 2023 Terrence Metz

ISBN: 9798753204561

DISCLAIMER

The publisher and the author make no guarantees concerning the level of success you may experience by following the advice and strategies contained in this book, and you accept the risk that results will differ for each individual. The examples and exercises provided in this book show exceptional results, which may not apply to the average reader, and are not intended to represent or guarantee that you will achieve the same or similar results.

v230208,y

Launching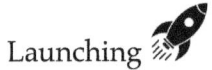

How to Use This Reader's Guide

This *Participant's Guide* is intended to be used alongside the book, *"Meetings That Get Results."* The book supports our curriculum and training programs designed to improve leadership, facilitation, and meeting design skills. The curriculum focuses on the skills required when leading groups to consensus. It includes a strong emphasis on servant leadership, planning sessions of all types, decision-making and prioritization, and creative problem-solving.

The culmination of 18 years of research, delivery, and practice providing over 15,000 hours of live instruction using *Certified* curriculum ensures that by reading the *Book* and using the *Guide*, you will be primed for leading successful business meetings:

> *"An engaging launch that transitions to a meeting design using proven procedures and tools, thus generating clear and actionable results that your participants will understand and own."*

We provide ample white space and encourage you to highlight, scribble, illustrate, take notes, and freely make this your personal copy, although use of our workbook is protected by copyright laws and restrictions, assignable to MG RUSH FACILITATION TRAINING.

Parts of this *Guide* include bonus material found only in the *Guide*. Additionally, with your alumni password, you can access hundreds of electronic documents, files, and support tools at:
https://mgrush.com/alumni-only-1932-2/

Our four-day online class or three-day in person classes can earn you CERTIFIED STRUCTURED FUNDAMENTALS FACILITATOR (CSFF) status. If you complete an additional two-day, in-person training and CAPSTONE, you may be awarded PROFESSIONAL FACILITATOR (CSPF) status.

As a Registered Educational Provider (REP) and Endorsed Education Provider (EEP), participants who successfully complete our CERTIFIED STRUCTURED PROFESSIONAL FACILITATOR [or FACILITATION FUNDAMENTALS] or {Agile Facilitation} qualify for:

1. *FAC CLPs* – Participants upon successful completion qualify for 40 [24] {20} Continuous Learning Points (CLPs) based on Federal Acquisition Certification Continuous Professional Learning Requirements using Training and Education activities.

2. *IIBA CDUs* – Participants upon successful completion qualify for 40 [24] {20} Continuing Development Units (CDUs) from the International Institute of Business Analysts, complying with BABOK® v2.0.

3. *SAVE CVS PDUs* – Participants upon successful completion qualify for 40 [24] {20} Professional Development Units (PDUs) from SAVE International®, complying with VMBOK® Facilitator Definition, Function Analysis System Technique (FAST) and supporting the eight Core Competencies of Team Facilitation, Section 3.1 (SAVE International® Core Competency Education Objectives and Testing Parameters for VMA and CVS).

4. *SCRUM SEUs* – Participants upon successful completion qualify for 40 [24] {20} SCRUM Educational Units (SEUs) from the SCRUM Alliance®, aligned with the Scrum Guide 2020.

5. The curriculum also confers 4.0 [2.4] {20} Continuing Educational Units (CEUs) for other professions.

Our curriculum fully aligns with learning objectives from the International Association of Facilitators (IAF) for submitting to their Certified Master Facilitator (CMF) testing and with facilitation skills enumerated by The International Institute For Facilitation (INIFAC).

Icons in the upper left match the table below, showing where you are in the *Participant's Guide* that corresponds to chapters in the book *"Meetings That Get Results."*

Table I.1. Meeting Design That Supports Servant Leadership

Chapter	Topic
1	***Serving:*** Resistance to change, importance of knowledge transfer, and the immense value of meetings based on clear thinking, servant leadership skills, and structured meeting design
2	***Leading:*** Critical disciplines including line of site, consciousness about different meeting roles, the nature of organizational alignment, and foundation of structure
3	***Facilitating:*** The indispensable servant skills that make it easier for meetings to get *DONE* faster through active listening, precise questioning, and timely challenging
4	***Collaborating:*** How to transform conflict into consensus leveraging the objectives of the product, project, department, business unit, and organization
5	***Structuring:*** Using a masterful *Launch* and *Wrap* for all sessions, modifying pre-built agendas and creating your own, and building fully scripted *Annotated Agendas* through structured conversations and vigorous preparation
6	***Planning:*** A fully integrated session that builds consensual plans about *who* does *what* by *when* to meet or exceed goals, key results, and other objectives
7	***Deciding:*** Proven *Tools* for galvanizing decisions and consensual agreement around purpose, criteria, options, and priorities throughout simple, complicated, and complex situations
8	***Solving:*** Field-tested *Meeting Approaches* and *Tools* using numerous creative activities for securing consensual agreement around innovative actions and solutions to embrace
9	***Controlling:*** Live and real-time sessions, hybrid in-person and online sessions, remote sessions, and virtual sessions and their differences. Support from "hip-pocket" *Intervention Tools* for special and unplanned meeting challenges
Appendix	***Supporting:*** Substantial and vital supplements such as the golden rule and the "silver rule," *Quick References*, and a list of *Tools* and where to find them, followed by a glossary and bibliography

Launching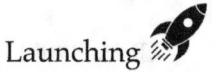

WORKSHOP PURPOSE

IS TO provide you the tools, tips, and technique

SO THAT you can lead people to make more informed decisions

WORKSHOP SCOPE

Teams and groups, meetings and workshops, and events and ceremonies

WORKSHOP OBJECTIVES

Leadership Consciousness
   "Knowing What DONE Looks Like"

Facilitative Competence
   "Reflecting the WHY Behind the WHAT"

Meeting Design Confidence
   "Procedural Structure, Method, and Tools"

OPERATIONAL (OE) EXCELLENCE MOMENT

The difference between being nice and being kind is that, while it is nice to be nice, it is essential to be kind.

BASIC AGENDA

- Launching & Serving
- Leading
- Facilitating
- Collaborating
- Decision-making
- Structuring
- Planning
- Problem-solving
- Controlling
- Practicing

Launching

Introduce Yourself

Use the following five topics to introduce yourself so that other participants get to know you better. Consider taking notes in advance so that you don't forget something important. Think of your responses as #revealing.

*Please NOTE: Your "ideal day" should be in your **personal** life, NOT at work.*

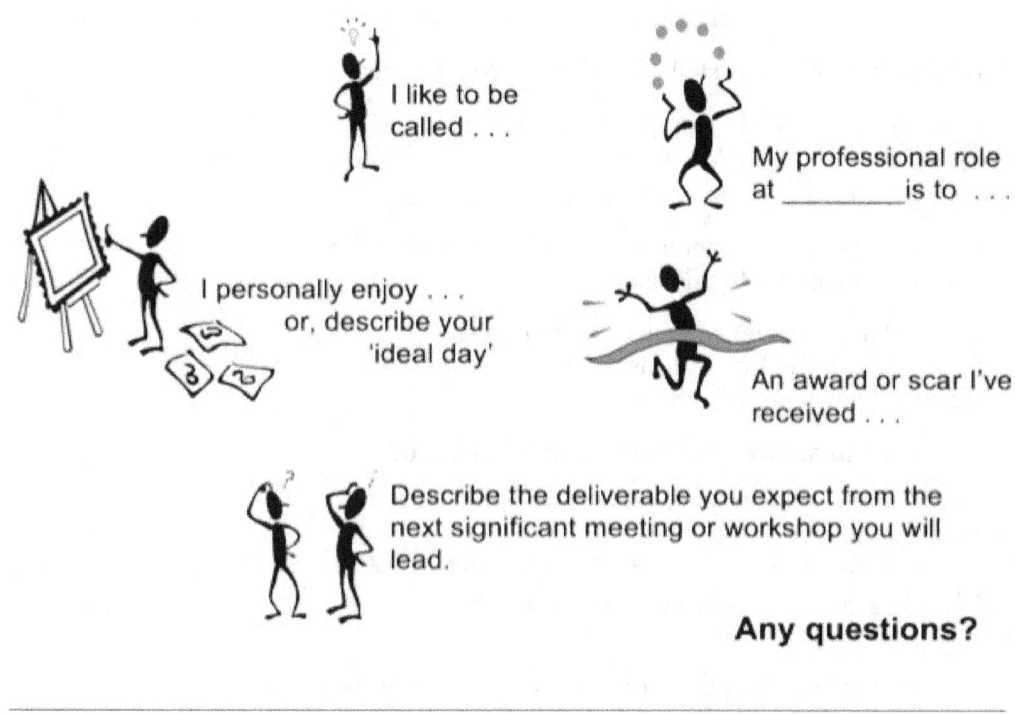

NOTES:

MG Rush Meeting Leadership Pre-Test

Test your wit in advance. Scientific American Mind has proven that pre-testing amplifies learning. While you may find some of the answers arguable, these questions will quickly set the tone for differences between "Facilitation" and "Presentation." Circle or note your best single response to each question, <u>prior to reading the book</u>.

QUESTIONS	NOTES & COMMENTS

A. Which trait is most effective for any type of leadership:
   1. Ability to describe WHERE the group is headed
   2. Knowledge to pre-determine WHICH path to take
   3. Experience knowing HOW to move a group of people
   4. Understanding WHY change is important

B. Describe the most effective type of decision-making:
   1. Answers can be best determined independent of the people affected by the decision
   2. Content and answers are clear and consistent, coming from the top and cascading down throughout an organization
   3. Content and answers flow freely in all directions
   4. Content and answers continuously bubble from the bottom and rise to the top

C. Which speaking skill contributes most to the effectiveness of a facilitator:
   1. Confidence building through a smooth and polished style
   2. Rhetorical precision and clarity of word choice
   3. Pleasing vocal qualities and tonal characteristics
   4. Personality or charisma that engages the audience

D. Which of the four steps of active listening is most critical to group understanding:
   1. Establishing contact with participants
   2. Absorbing the content participants provide
   3. Reflection of the content offered by participants
   4. Confirmation that content reflection was accurate

E. What challenges facilitators most frequently when asking questions:

Launching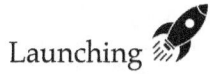

QUESTIONS

1. Asking questions in an optimal sequence
2. Asking questions so broad that participants find it difficult to respond
3. Not asking clearly for the content that is required
4. Pausing long enough to wait for responses

F. The most common violation of facilitator neutrality:

1. Cheerleading, encouraging participants by praising "good" or "great" ideas
2. Espousing one's own opinion, opining on content
3. Judging participant input to be weak, frail, or insufficient
4. Providing examples using the subject matter experts' content and experience

G. Most business meetings fail because . . .

1. Agendas are poorly constructed, if at all—and then they are not followed
2. Meeting purpose, scope, and deliverables are unclear, or poor at best
3. Meetings start well but finish poorly, if at all—most meetings end but don't finish
4. The facilitators avoid conflict and frequently rush to the *Parking Lot* rather than facilitate argumentation around topics and disagreements that require neutral guidance

Meetings That Get Results — Participant's Guide©

Serving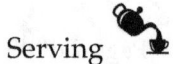

Serving

A. *'Facilitaere'* means _____ _____ _____.

B. Use the <u>same</u> word to fill in both blanks below:

- Management means doing things _____.
- Leadership means doing the _____ things.

C. **Identify** the proper <u>sequence</u> for seven activities of a professional, structured meeting or workshop launch:

Optimal Sequence	Activity
1.	A. Administrivia
2.	B. Basic Agenda
3.	C. Ground Rules
4.	D. Meeting Deliverables
5.	E. Meeting Purpose
6.	F. Meeting Scope
7.	G. Roles and Impact

D. **Explain Consensus**:

1. What does it mean to say, "I can live with it," *professionally*?
   _____
   _____

2. What does it mean to say, "I can live with it," *personally*?
   _____
   _____

3. What does duty or 'fiduciary responsibility' imply for meeting participants?
   _____
   _____

Serving

E. Which significant, two-word *Ground Rule* should always be added to online meetings and workshops.

_____ _____

F. Transformation efforts are affected by the FUD factor, that stands for . . .

F = _____

U = _____

D = _____

G. Empirical evidence shows that 'Nobody is smarter than everybody' because . . .

_____
_____
_____

H. People don't actually change their minds, but they do . . .

_____
_____
_____

I. The three common types of meetings we focus on include:

1. _____

2. _____

3. _____

J. Meeting leadership is about leading with _____ that are properly _____ while always providing a _____ environment for everybody's response.

Meetings That Get Results — Participant's Guide©

Leading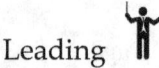

What Does DONE Look Like?

Flag on this page so you can refer to it quickly.

Organizational Holarchy of Alignment

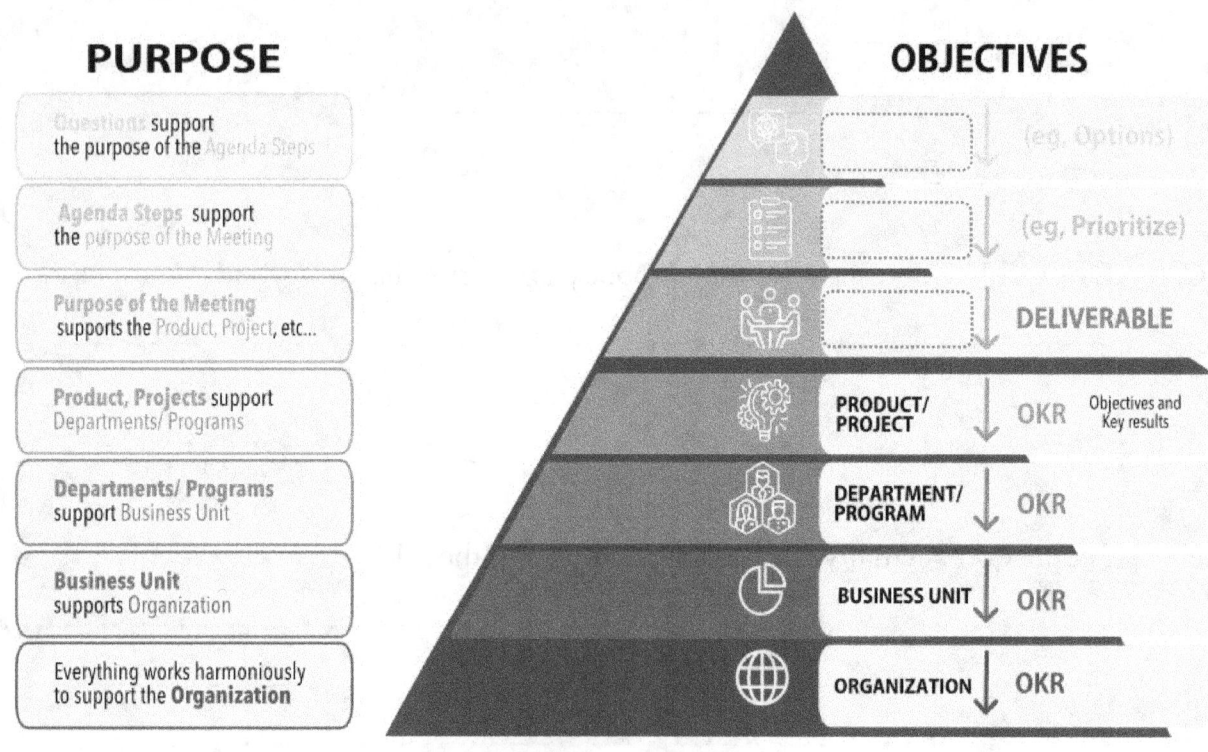

Structure: The Conversion of Thoughts Into Actions
(Transformation of the abstract into the concrete)

Fill in the top row summarizing the three stages of structured transformation.

Level of Structure / Technique			
Apocryphal	Thoughts	Words	Deeds
Logic	Why	What	How
Life Cycle	Planning	Analysis	Design
Plato	Logic	Rhetoric	Grammar
Logic	Why	What	How
Use Case	Input	Process	Output

Meetings That Get Results — Participant's Guide©

Leading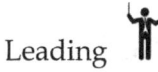

Accountabilities and Responsibilities in Meetings

Using the icons, identify the seven accountabilities in meetings. Highlight, check, circle, or indicate the four accountabilities normally performed by the meeting leader.

1.

2.

3.

4.

7.

5.

6.

Meetings That Get Results — Participant's Guide©

What Does DONE Look Like? or, "Right-to-Left" Thinking Exercise

Exercise Goals
- To demonstrate that for effective leadership, nothing is more important than knowing where you are going.
- To become conscious of the distinction between the meeting and the initiative it supports.
- To help you identify the right source for meeting design assistance.
- To emphasize the importance of being conscious about meeting roles and representing all stakeholders.
- To encourage students to consider *pro bono* engagements to practice their approach and tools that can be used during structured meetings and workshops.

Instructions
Students will separate into groups assigned by the instructor to:
- Define one or two different meetings or workshops not related to your profession or to each other. Situations must be nonprofessional such as social or organizational situations where consensus is important or challenging. Consider meeting or workshops such as planning (ie, WHO does WHAT and WHEN), analysis (eg, prioritization, problem solving, or 'requirements'), or design (ie, HOW TO).
- Each team will orally explain the purpose of their workshop; ie, how does it support the objective of the project it supports.
- Using large Post-It paper or other visible means, write down and prepare to present the following in the sequence shown.
    - *Deliverable* (with some detail — what does it look like?)
    - Identify your *meeting designer*[s] (ie, expert[s] for the providing the approach and questions that build your deliverable).
    - *Who* and *how many* of each type of participant will be invited to the meeting?
- Determine who will provide the primary voice presenting the situations for your group.

Notes:

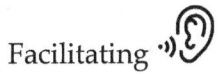

Context vs. Content

Indicate which of the following are Content (**C**) or Context (**X**).

1. _____ "Can we break for lunch?"
2. _____ "Can't we use the multi-colored voting dots?"
3. _____ "I think the gift we provide should be memorable."
4. _____ "Now we are going to use the *PowerBalls Tool*."
5. _____ "Should we wait for Jim?"
6. _____ "Shouldn't we cover the criteria first?"
7. _____ "What are our competitors doing about this?"
8. _____ "Who is going to buy the gift?"
9. _____ "With leadership support, we can exceed objectives within ten months."

Rhetorical Precision (Clarity)

Which of the following are True (**T**) or False (**F**)?

1. _____ A facilitator's four core disciplines include speaking clearly, asking precise questions, listening critically, and remaining neutral.
2. _____ Dictionaries should be consulted to resolve arguments.
3. _____ Facilitators should challenge speakers when participants react with uncertainty.
4. _____ Facilitators should not pause too long. Quiet time should be avoided.
5. _____ Facilitators should probe the word choice of speakers.
6. _____ Getting the 'right' words is more important than using icons or symbols.
7. _____ It's OK for a facilitator to say "uhm."
8. _____ People are frequently in violent agreement with each other, defining terms differently or using different terms to describe the same thing.
9. _____ Removing distractions remains the most important duty of facilitators.
10. _____ Vibrant, captivating, and charismatic facilitators are highly desired.

Facilitating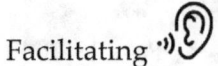

Questioning: Your Powerful Traction Device

Challenging participants to think clearly requires both art (not offending the subject matter expert) and science (pushing on the objective proof supporting their remarks).

Therefore:

1. What type of questions should usually be avoided?

   _____ _____

2. What six-word question challenges modifiers (eg, adjectives and adverbs)?

   _____ ____ _____ _____ ____ _____

3. What magical three-word question will we learn this afternoon?

   ____ _____ _____

4. For transitions, what three questions may be effectively substituted for "Are we OK with this list?" or "Any more?" (pg 185)

   A - _____

   B - _____

   C - _____

Active Listening: Listening is More Persuasive than Speaking

List the four activities required of active listening (pg. 52):

1. _____
2. _____
3. _____
4. _____

Meetings That Get Results — Participant's Guide©

Neutrality: Indispensable Trait of Professional Facilitators

Which of the following are True (**T**) or False (**F**)?

1. _____ During critical, facilitated session the USA Joint Chiefs of Staff wear their full regalia, badges, and awards to make sure nobody forgets who is superior.

2. _____ If you are 'dying' to add content, it's OK to tell participants that you will share your opinions with them after the meeting.

3. _____ If you must praise your group, praise the quantity or velocity of their contributions but not the quality.

4. _____ It's OK to switch roles mid-stream and pass judgement on content or to add new content.

5. _____ Neutrality demands that you are not passionate about the meeting or workshop.

6. _____ Professional facilitators do not need to be content experts, only content conversant.

7. _____ The fastest way to get a group of people to go quiet is to violate neutrality.

8. _____ The number one behavior most people could embrace immediately to make themselves better facilitators is to stop using the first-person singular, "I."

9. _____ When facilitating, it's counter-intuitive but true, but you're better off telling someone their idea is 'really bad' rather than saying they had a 'good' or 'great idea.'

Facilitating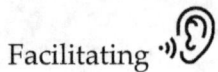

Listening Lab Exercise

Exercise Goals
To demonstrate how clear speaking, active listening, disciplined questions, meaningful challenges, neutrality, and observation support effective facilitation.

Exercise Instructions
Everyone leads a brief discussion (see below for ideas).
- One volunteer at a time (ie, the facilitator)
- All else are participants pretending to be subject matter experts
- After the session, all offer up comments and questions as students

Exercise Roles
- *Facilitator*—set the context that you are seeking improved understanding about the groups' experience, facts, and evidence regarding (insert topic). Use active listening and probing questions while listening to the participants. Challenge assumptions and ask for ways to measure their fuzzy terms like "a lot." Demand evidence that supports their reasons. Feed back and confirm to assure that you are getting it "right" according to the speaker's standards.
  - Avoid stringing together more than one question at a time.
  - Interrupt a long-winded speaker to enable interim feedback and confirmation.
- *Participants*—respond with any thoughts you care to offer up—views do not necessarily need to agree with your actual views.
  - Provide a simple "yes", "no", or "maybe" if asked a close-ended question.
- *Comments*—focus on the facilitator. Note what they do well and when they violate the principles of active listening. Time-permitting, share your observations with the entire group during the session review.

Each round typically lasts five minutes—until you hear the timer. Participants share their observations for the benefit of the facilitator and offer up questions about each session. The exercise continues until every participant has had an opportunity to perform as facilitator.

Possible Topics

- Bitcoin-cryptocurrency-chain block
- Change start time for High School students until 9:00AM
- Concealed weapons
- Gun free zones
- Legalized gambling
- No cellular telephone use in motorized vehicles
- Seat belt laws
- Super-stars as role models
- Vaccinations

- Capital punishment
- Climatic weather changes
- Dress codes in schools
- Immigration policies
- Motorcycle helmet laws
- Citizenship for children born in the USA with illegal parents
- Spanking children
- Telecommuting employees
- Vegetarianism

- Change the legal "drinking" age to match the Armed Forces age
- Compulsory adult community service
- eCigarette usage in public spaces
- Legalization of marijuana
- NCAA college playoff expansion
- Prohibition of alcohol
- Stem cell research
- Teacher pay (eg, salary) in America
- *or, something of your own choosing*

Meetings That Get Results — Participant's Guide©

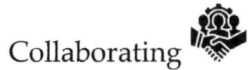

Collaborating
Individual Thinking Styles

Draw three straight lines, without crossing, to connect the four dots. Do not pick up your pen once you start. You must end up where you started (here are four separate sets for experimenting).

There are four volumes of Goethe on the shelf.

The total pages of each volume are five cm. thick.

The front and rear covers of each are one-half of one cm. thick each.

A bookworm starts eating at page one of volume one and eats straight through to the last page of volume four.

How far does it travel?

Individual Behavior

A. In two words, explain the Rosetta Stone of Facilitation:

   _____ _____

B. What is the primary rule for managing dysfunctional participants?

   _____ _____ _____

C. Which four (in person) or five (online) Ground Rules are critical?

   1. _____

   2. _____

   3. _____

   4. _____

   5. _____

D. Name five activities that help secure input from quieter (all) people:

Activity
1.
2.
3.
4.
5.

Collaborating

Behavior Matching (Insert the letter from "What to Do" in the link column)

WHAT TO DO	LINK	TITLE
1A. Interview your participants 1B. *Breakout Teams* 1C. Non-verbal solicitation 1D. Reinforce during break 1E. Round-robins & Post-it® note techniques		A Can't Stay (Leaves early)
2 Enforce the 'No Hiding' *Ground Rule* for online participants. When in person, walk around the room or take a quick ergonomic break.		B Cliquer (Side conversations)
3 Explain and enforce the role of *Observer*, noting that *Observer* may speak during breaks or after the session has completed.		C Controller (Back seat driver)
4 First get the original speaker to confirm you received their input correctly and then offer this person time to add their own point of view.		D Disapprover (Non-verbal)
5 Interrupt them immediately to protect the person interrupted but do not forget to get back to them. Impatience is preferred over apathy.		E Disengaged (Electronic leashes)
6 Listen first, however, never turn over control. Talk to them during breaks. Enforce scope carefully to avoid scope creep.		F Genius (Know-it-all)
7 Move near the _____. Direct open hands to them seeking valid, counter positions. Give online participants the option of saying "pass" if called upon.		G Impatient (Interrupter)
8 Record input if in scope of the question at hand. If not in scope, ask them to write it down so they don't forget it when you turn to them later.		H Monopolizer (Dominator)
9 Stand between two people. Immediately interrupt personal attacks. Mute online attackers. Make sure comments remain professional and not personal.		I Quiet Person
10 Standing close to _____ will stop their conversation. Enforce 'One Conversation at a Time' *Ground Rule*. Also enforce if you sense too much private online chatting.		J Repeater
11 The _____ needs to understand that their point of view has been captured. Document their input. Show them visually that 'you got it.' When they begin to repeat themselves, interrupt them and read back what you have, asking them "What would you like to add?"		K Skeptic
12 They may have a legitimate reason such as another meeting, day care pickup, or van pool departure. Understand constraints before the meeting begins and schedule accordingly.		L Snoozer
13 Enforce 'Be Here Now' *Ground Rule*. Allow frequent bio-breaks, especially when online, for people to respond to bodily needs and electronic leashes.		M Spinner (Twister)
14 Use 50-minute meeting intervals to allow people some transition time between back-to-back meetings. Enforce 'Be Here Now' and 'No Hiding' *Ground Rules*.		N Tardy
15 Use laser focus so that they know you see them. During breaks, talk to them. Do NOT publicly call out their name. For online violators, send them a private chat.		O Uninvited
16 Use the 'What—So What—Now What' (*Content Management*, pg 258) tool. Use conversations in advance of the meeting to anticipate when they should speak up and provide them with an optimal time to bring up their concern(s).		P Verbal Attacker
17 Writing down their input fully will satisfy them. Interrupt them if they repeat, reading back to them what you have.		Q Workaholic (Busybody)

Meetings That Get Results — Participant's Guide©

Collaborating

Group Behavior

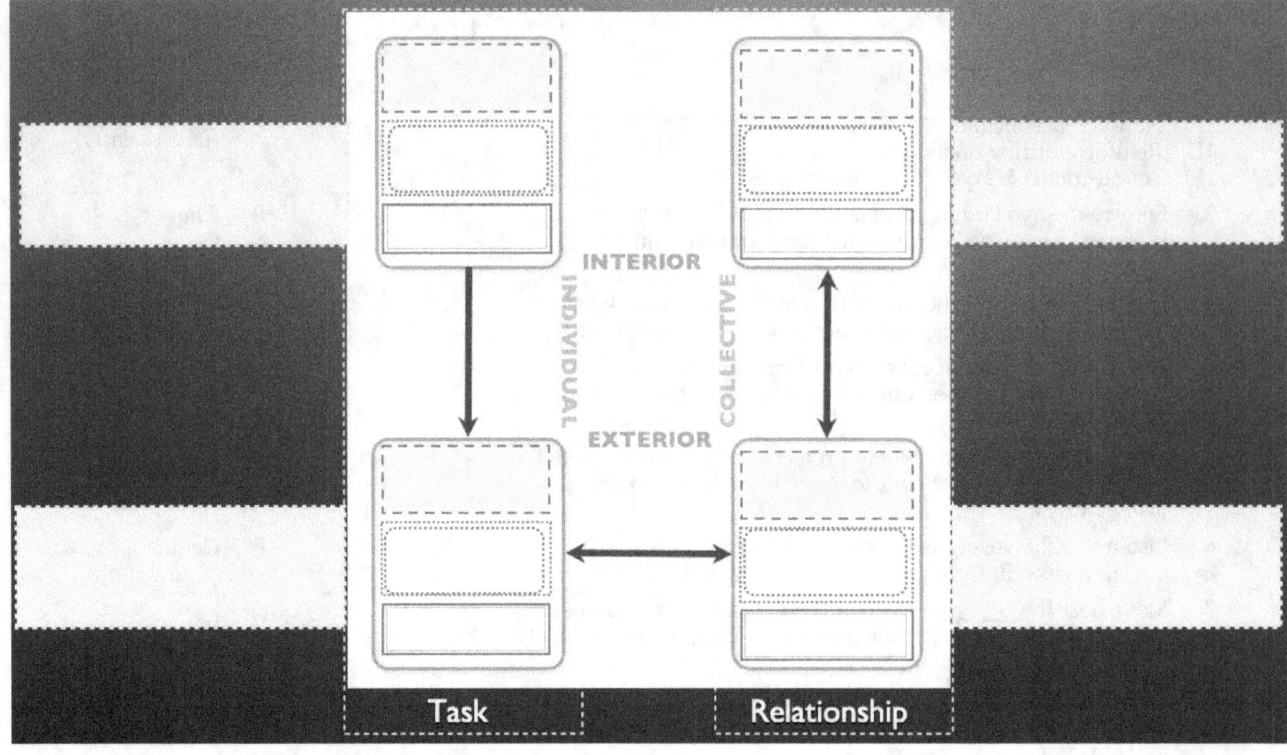

Argument Resolution:
Four Activities to Manage Meeting Arguments

NOTE: It is NOT your responsibility to _____ conflict,

It is your responsibility to _____ it.

Four Sequential Actions for Managing Conflict
1.
2.
3.
4.

Meetings That Get Results — Participant's Guide©

Decision-making

We all work for the same manager (Sally) who is very well liked by the entire organization. After 35 years, she is retiring next month. We want to give her a very special "going away" gift. What do we agree to get her?

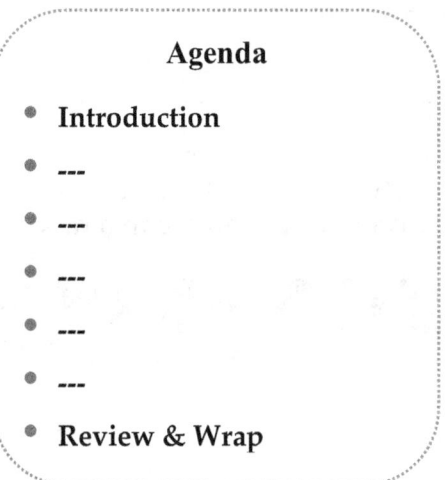

Purpose Tool (pg 184)

Definition Tool (pg 152)
Easy to build, consensual definitions optimally include five traits (attributes):

Powerful Definition Attributes
1.
2.
3.
4.
5.

Meetings That Get Results — Participant's Guide©

Deciding

Procedures and Tools

Insert the three terms specific to *Brainstorming* representing the Trichotomy (pg 132).

(Clue)	WILL	WISDOM	ACTIVITY
(Universal Friendly)			
	Fact	Implication	Recommendation

Identify the two rules that are paramount during the <u>Listing</u> activity of *Brainstorming* (or nearly any other time you are in a mode of capturing ideas from participants).

Two Sacrosanct Ideation Rules
1.
2.

PowerBalls

Iconic Prioritization (pg 191 – 192)

Illustrate using appropriate icon	Define Hi, Low, and Moderate (using two-word economic explanations)
	High/ Full/ Frequent
	Low/ Empty/ Rarely
	Moderate/ Half-full/ Occasionally

Back and Forth, *Book-end Rhetoric (pg 193)*

LEAST	MOST
Which of these is least important?	Which of these is most important?
Which of the remaining is **NEXT** least important?	Which of the remaining is **NEXT** most important?
Which of the remaining is **NEXT** least important?	Which of the remaining is **NEXT** most important?

Meetings That Get Results — Participant's Guide©

Meeting Pathway

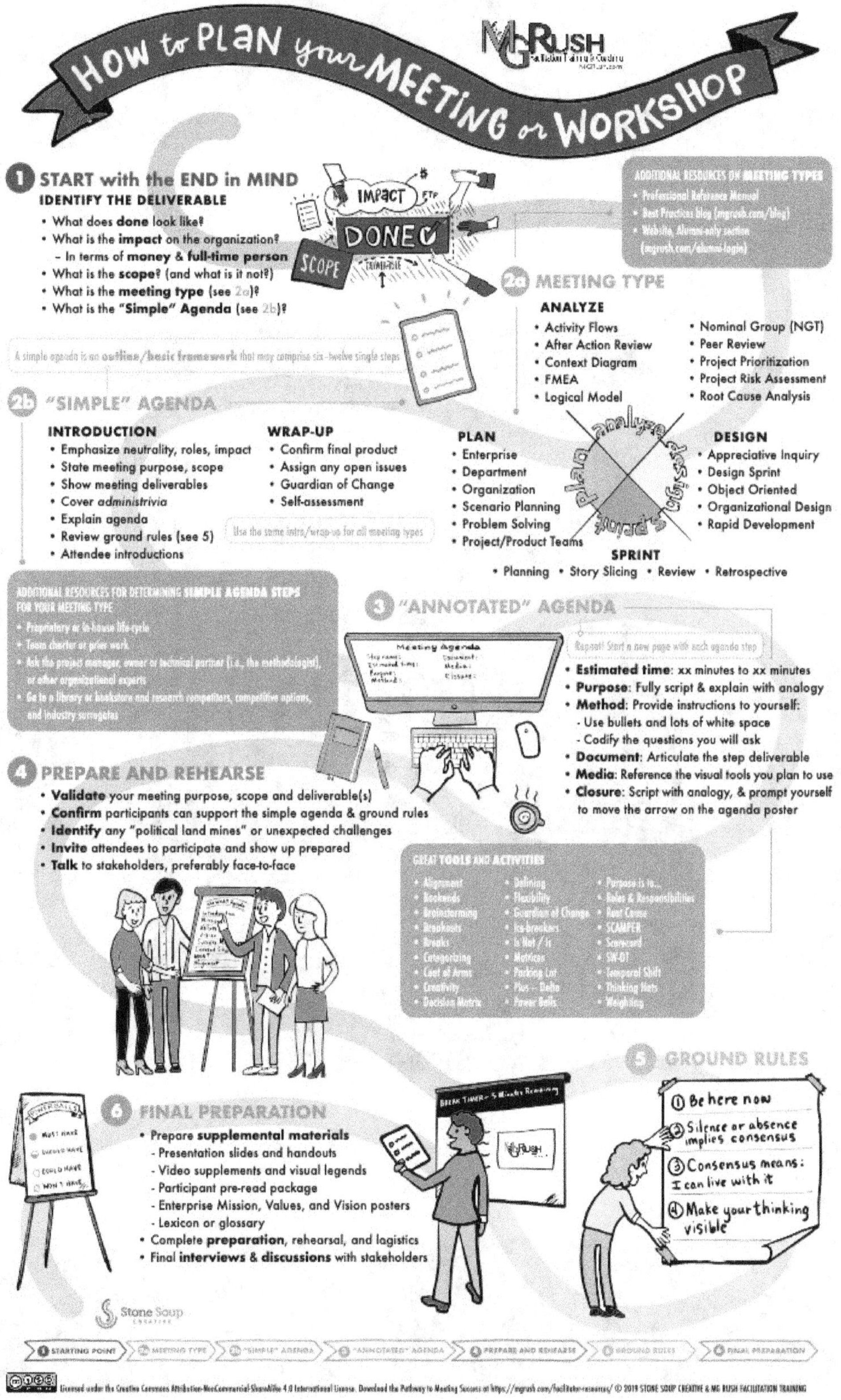

Workshop Canvass

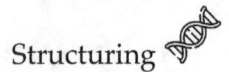

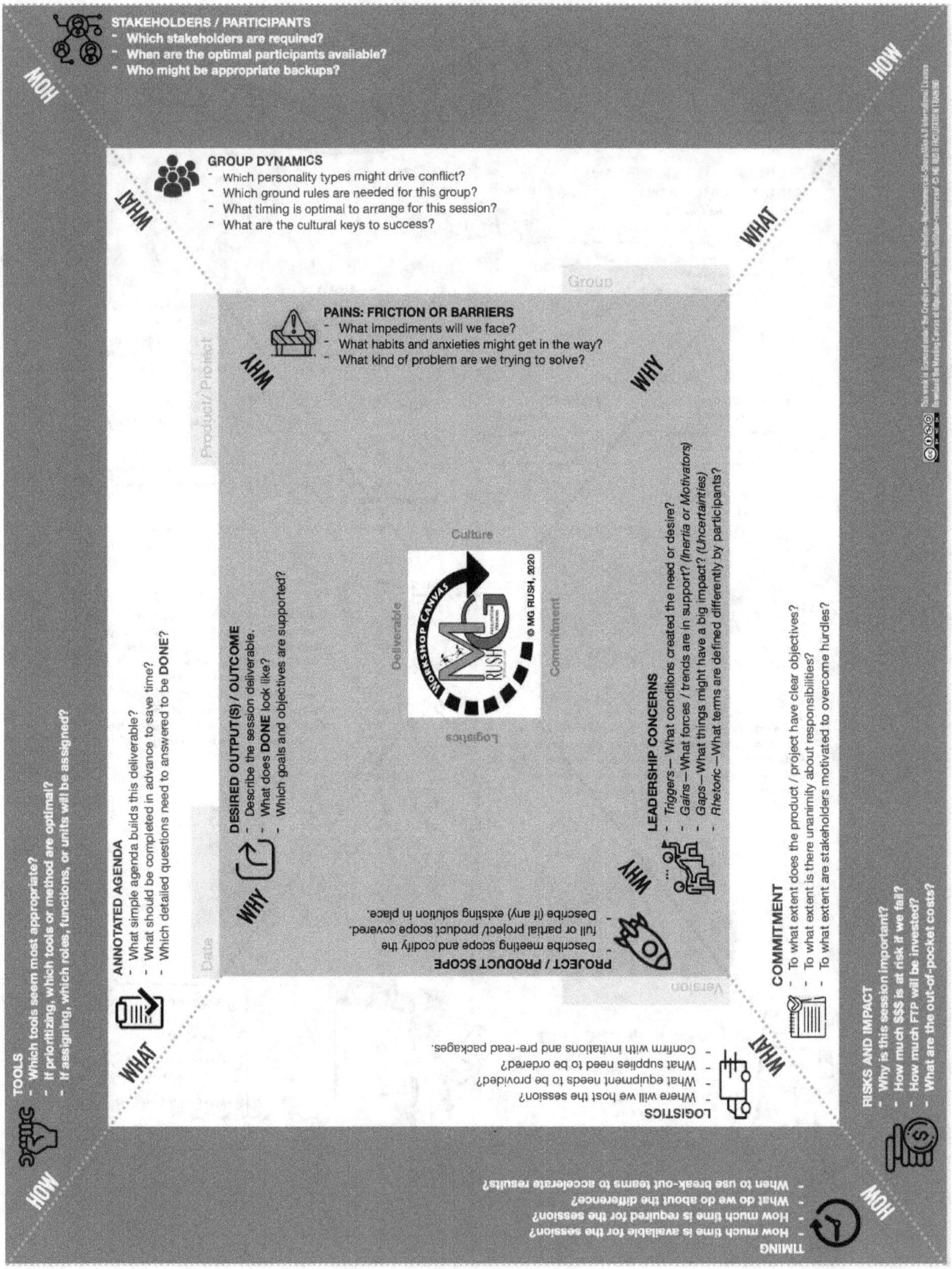

STAKEHOLDERS / PARTICIPANTS
- Which stakeholders are required?
- When are the optimal participants available?
- Who might be appropriate backups?
HOW
HOW
GROUP DYNAMICS
- Which personality types might drive conflict?
- Which ground rules are needed for this group?
- What timing is optimal to arrange for this session?
- What are the cultural keys to success?
WHAT
WHAT
PAINS: FRICTION OR BARRIERS
- What impediments will we face?
- What habits and anxieties might get in the way?
- What kind of problem are we trying to solve?
WHY
WHY
Group
Product/ Project
Culture
Deliverable
Commitment
Logistics
Data
Version
© MG RUSH, 2020
WORKSHOP CANVAS
TOOLS
- Which tools seem most appropriate?
- If prioritizing, which tools or method are optimal?
- If assigning, which roles, functions, or units will be assigned?
ANNOTATED AGENDA
- What simple agenda builds this deliverable?
- What should be completed in advance to save time?
- Which detailed questions need to answered to be DONE?
DESIRED OUTPUT(S) / OUTCOME
- Describe the session deliverable.
- What does DONE look like?
- Which goals and objectives are supported?
LEADERSHIP CONCERNS
- Triggers—What conditions created the need or desire?
- Gains—What forces / trends are in support? (Inertia or Motivators)
- Gaps—What things might have a big impact? (Uncertainties)
- Rhetoric—What terms are defined differently by participants?
COMMITMENT
- To what extent does the product / project have clear objectives?
- To what extent is there unanimity about responsibilities?
- To what extent are stakeholders motivated to overcome hurdles?
RISKS AND IMPACT
- Why is this session important?
- How much $$$ is at risk if we fail?
- How much FTP will be invested?
- What are the out-of-pocket costs?
PROJECT / PRODUCT SCOPE
- Describe meeting scope and codify the full or partial project / product scope covered.
- Describe (if any) existing solution in place.
LOGISTICS
- Where will we host the session?
- What equipment needs to be provided?
- What supplies need to be ordered?
- Confirm with invitations and pre-read packages.
TIMING
- How much time is available for the session?
- How much time is required for the session?
- What do we do about the difference?
- When to use break-out teams to accelerate results?
WHY
WHY
WHAT
WHAT
HOW
HOW

Two Agenda Types

1. **Basic Agenda** --- a traditional list with NOUNS ONLY (here is an *illustrative* example using the archetype for decision-making):
   - Launch
   - Purpose of the Object
   - Options
   - Criteria
   - Deselection and Decision
   - Testing
   - Wrap

2. **Annotated Agenda** --- a fully scripted plan for everything you do or say. Most of our *Annotated Agendas* run between fifteen and twenty-five pages. Also see your "Class Supplements" (Girl's Inc.) PDF package for an example and "The Meeting Pathway and Workshop Canvass" PDF (prior pages) for additional support.

Introduction or Launch

A. What is the optimal sequence for your seven introductory activities?

Introductory Activity
1.
2.
3.
4.
5.
6.
7.

Structuring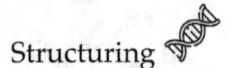

B. What is the optimal sequence for your four review and wrap activities?

Review & Wrap Activity
1.
2.
3.
4.

Icebreakers, Open Issues, and Assessment

Icebreakers (pg 97)
Icebreakers may also be used as warm-ups to *Creativity* or team-building in the middle of a session. Some of my favorites include:
- Describe the situation surrounding a scar you received or an award you earned.
- Mad, Sad, and Glad
- NASA's "Stuck on the Moon" scenario

Open Issues or Parking Lot (pg 102 - 103)
Identify three styles, modes, or tools you might use to manage open issues:

Issue Types	Tool Name or Procedure
Simple/ Quick	
Complicated/ Moderate	
Complex/ Who knows?	

Meetings That Get Results — Participant's Guide©

Structuring

Assessment Options (pg 104 - 105)
Four procedures that may be used to solicit input about the session and the session leader performance.

Frequency and Speed	Tool Name or Procedure
Frequent / Quick	
Seldom / Quickest	
Occasionally / Quick	
Optimal / Thoughtful	

Annotated Agenda

Label the six components of an *Annotated Agenda* for <u>each</u> *Agenda Step*. Remember to always begin a new page and repeat for each and every step in your agenda.

Component Label	STEP NAME Comments
1.	Script --- optimally include your metaphor.
2.	Preferably a range and not a fixed number.
3.	- Detail procedure and *Tool* - Use bullets and lots of white space - Stipulate precise questions to be asked
4.	What does DONE look like from the step?
5.	Indicate visual support such as definition slide, iconic legend, or other charts and slides
6.	Script --- optimally include your metaphor.

Meetings That Get Results — Participant's Guide©

Structuring

Complete Cookbook Agendas That Alumni Can Download

Planning Agendas	Analysis Agendas	Design Agendas
Planning [Strategic or Team]	After Action Review (Hot Wash)	Basic Design Agenda
Project Planning	Sprint Review	Design Sprint (Google)
Problem Solving	Context Diagram	Transaction (JAD)
Scenario Planning	Activity Flows [Requirements]	Organizational Design
Sprint Planning	Failure Mode & Effect Analysis	Object-Oriented Design
Strategy Mapping	Logical Model	Resource Life-Cycle
Decision Support	Peer Review Inspection	Sales Force Realignment
Resource Life Cycle	Data Flow Diagram	TRIZ
New Thinking	Knowledge Management	Win-Win
Appreciative Inquiry	Project Prioritization	Basic Design Agenda
	Wright's "494"	Design Sprint (Google)

Participant Conversations

A. After asking for permission to take notes use the following, with few (if any) modifications or changes to the words used or the sequence provided.

   1. "What do you _____ from the session?"

   2. "What will make the workshop a complete _____?"

   3. "What should the _____ look like?"

   4. "What _____ do you foresee?"

   5. Confirm who should attend the workshop? Who should not? Why?

   6. "What is going to be my biggest _____?"

   7. "Does the meeting deliverable and agenda make sense to you?"

   8. "Are the 'electronic leashes' and 'consensus' _____ acceptable?"

   9. "What _____ do you think we should answer?"

   10. "What should I have asked that I didn't _____?"

Meetings That Get Results — Participant's Guide©

Structuring

B. After preparing your annotated agenda, distribute a *Participant's Package* for your critical events and workshops. Include <u>each of the following</u> in every package.

1. _____ purpose, scope, deliverable, and agenda

2. Lexicon or _____

3. _____ mission, values, vision, and objectives

4. _____ team charter or _____ vision

Large Group Set-ups

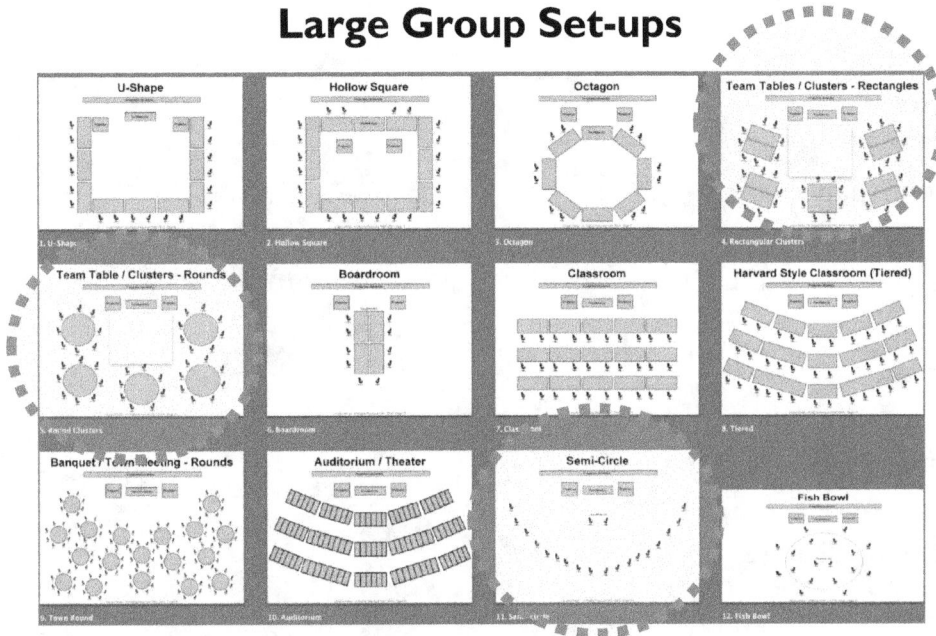

Agenda Steps and Tools

What does the deliverable from any agenda step look like?

Examples of What Agenda Step Deliverables Might Look Like	
• 3-D Printed Solution	• Coat of Arms
• Decision Matrix	• DQ Spider
• Iconic Matrix	• Illustration
• Infographic	• List
• Mathematical Diagram (eg, Scatter Plot)	• Narrative Statements
• Numeric Matrix	• Pages
• Paragraph	• Perceptual Map
• Prioritized List	• RASI Chart
• Run-on Sentence	• Sentence
• Spreadsheet	• Storyboard
• Template	• Wireframe
• Working Code	• Etc.

Meetings That Get Results — Participant's Guide©

Planning Agendas

Define each planning agenda step below by the primary question it answers.

Agenda Step	Primary Question Answered
Mission	
Values	
Vision	
Measures	
Situation Analysis	
Actions	
Alignment	
Assignments	
Guardian of Change	

Mission & Coat of Arms

1. Stress the importance of _____. If people cannot remember the *Mission* expression, it's worthless.

2. A _____ is worth a thousand pictures.

3. The *Creativity Tool* leverages one question and seeks many answers (One-to-Many). Whereas the _____ ____ _____ *Tool* provides the opportunity to use many questions and secure at least one answer per question (Many-to-One).

4. If you are using the *Coat of Arms Tool (pg 139)* for a *Mission* expression, bias yourself toward the _____ for showing up, rather than the MBA questions.

Meetings That Get Results — Participant's Guide©

Planning

Values & Categorizing

Categorizing (pg 142)
This tool represents the heart and soul and logic for taking initial input, conducting analysis, and refining the final output.

1. _____ _____ represent the symptoms behind causes.

2. Don't forget, "Does this new statement also capture the _____ of something else up here that is not <u>underscored</u>?"

3. At all times, especially with *Breakout Teams (pg 138)*, discard all of the _____ _____ and build new sheets.

Vision & Temporal Shift

Temporal Shift (pg 147)

1. Fill in the both blanks with the same word:

    "You are on a beach in Aruba, five years from now. As you grab this magazine, behold the _____ is about the legacy you left behind beginning with the work you began today. What does the _____ say?"

2. Calculate the _____ _____ _____ _____ based on when the group has disbanded.

3. With four people or more, always use _____ _____ to get input.

4. *Temporal Shift* provides the perfect opportunity for tactile stimulation if you distribute copies of a _____.

Measures & Scorecard

1. Most critically, link your *Measures (pg 148)* back to the _____. These are indicators as to the amount of progress being made to reach the _____.

2. Do not initially demand specific criteria. People don't think _____. They think DUMB (Dull, Ubiquitous, Myopic, and Broad).

Meetings That Get Results — Participant's Guide©

Measurement Test
S =
M =
A =
R =
T =

Current Situation and Quantitative TO-WS Analysis

Quantitative TO-WS Analysis (pg 152 - 161)

Externally Uncontrollable
T =
O =

Internally Controllable
W =
S =

1. Never let a group define an internally controllable _____ as an <u>Opportunity</u> for improvement.

2. Begin with the external _____ and then _____, before identifying internal <u>Weaknesses</u> and <u>Strengths</u>.

Five Ways to Signify Meaning
1. Ill =
2. Nar =
3. Num =
4. Non =
5. Sym =

Planning

Actions

1. The TO-WS spreadsheet reflects the _____ _____, albeit numerically.
2. Conduct a TO-WS Analysis, not because MBA say to, rather to build consensual understanding that leads to interpretation and conversion of what _____ the numbers represent. Complete the translation, using the numbers as a guide to the level of importance.
3. Encourage integrative attitudes and rhetoric. It's not "Perspective One" <u>OR</u> "Perspective Two." Rather, it's "Perspective One" <u>AND</u> "Perspective Two."

Alignment

Alignment **Agenda Step**
Convert impotent rhetoric into a highly potent force by using open-ended questions. Memorize the following and then tattoo it to your left forearm so that you don't forget the three magical words . . .

"_____ _____ _____? *(does it)*"

Alignment (pg 167)
This step is fun. Your hard work is over. Simply build a *Decision Matrix* that arrays your options (*Actions*) against your criteria (*Measures*).

1. The critical 'must do' is to revisit each *Measure*, one at a time, and ask the question: "Do we have enough _____ to ensure that we reach this *Measure*?" (for each and every *Measure*).

2. If yes, move on to the next *Measure*. If not, return to the _____ _____ to determine what other *Action*(s) should be embraced to reach that specific *Measure*.

Meetings That Get Results — Participant's Guide©

Planning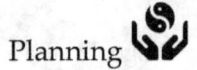

Assignments

Roles and Responsibilities (pg 168 - 172)
With over twenty documented versions of RASI, use either RASI or the version best suited for your culture to combine the WHO with the WHAT.

Roles and Responsibilities
R =
A =
S =
I =

1. Footnote the "_____" if they are paying for all of the *Actions*.
2. One and only one, big, red "_____" per *Action*.
3. Time-permitting, allow zero or many _____ and _____ for each *Action*.

Guardian of Change

Guardian of Change **Agenda Step**
Unique, practical, and powerful --- let's agree on what we are going to tell people we got done in this meeting so that it sounds like we were in the same meeting together.

Communications Plan (pg 173 - 174)
Once you understand that groups cannot focus on "many-to-many," simply extend the "one-to-many" as many times as it takes.

Convert the following letter clues into full words.

Communications Plan
Identify Sta . . . =
For each Sta . . . list Mes . . . =
For each Mes . . . list Veh . . . =
For each Veh . . . list Fre . . . =

Meetings That Get Results — Participant's Guide©

Solving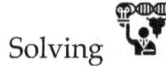

Problem-solving
Procedures and Tools

Situation
Our cyber security technicians are burnt out. We need to avoid burnout because our department depends on qualified technicians and satisfied customers. What are the elements we should consider and what does the deliverable look like?

Deliverable

Agenda
- Introduction
- ---
- ---
- ---
- ---
- ---
- Review & Wrap

Perspectives

Pushing on *Perspectives (pg 226 - 230)*

- Six M's List the "M" Drivers
- Seven P's List the "P" Drivers
- Five S's List the "S" Drivers

Seven Thinking Hats

Impose perspective to drive creative solutions. Insert the letter from "Description" in the link column corresponding to the color of the *Six Hats* (plus one).

Description		Link	Seven Hats
A	Focuses on questioning and defining the evidence, facts, and information that others consider objective in nature.	1	Black
B	Gives permission and encouragement to forward feelings and hunches without fully justifying them.	2	Blue
C	Looks not at the method itself used for building, managing, and concluding the process, including using and sequencing the other hats.	3	Green
D	Makes us consider the risks and impact involved -- why something may not work, why it may be illegal, or various means it may go wrong.	4	Royal
E	Encourages creative, "out-of-the-box" proposals, suggestions, ideas, alternatives, and the unforeseen.	5	Red
F	Perspective of the owner who is committed and invested in the meeting output and project outcome. May have difficulty switching perspectives because they own the results.	6	White
G	Why you think something will work; the upside, savings, benefits, and advantages; usually forward-thinking, positive, and optimistic.	7	Yellow

Online and Other Meeting Support

A. *Online Meeting Warnings:*
   - **WARNING**: Online meetings do _____ substitute for face-to-face
   - **WARNING**: _____ __ _____ meetings are helpful when challenging issues, arguments, or disagreements must be resolved. In-person meetings are also helpful when people are experiencing job assignment, information, organizational, or technology overload

B. *Significant Online Meeting Considerations:*
   1. All or _____ (co-location)
   2. Allow for _____ _____.
   3. Always enforce a _____.
   4. Call on _____ participants or offices first.
   5. Create a _____ seating arrangement.
   6. Don't skip the _____ _____.
   7. Everyone should _____ their electronic leashes.
   8. Frequently use _____ _____ sessions.
   9. Make sure that everyone feels comfortable saying _____ at any time.
   10. Remain conscious about 3-second _____.

C. *Other Meeting Tips and Types:*
   1. If you or the participants are burned out, take a _____ (pg 256).
   2. The transformation from abstract ideas into concrete actions is served well by the _____ _____ tool (pg 258).
   3. _____ meetings might use the three-question approach (pg 262).
   4. *Robert's Rules of Order* are used for _____ _____ (pg 263).

Bridging

Matching (Insert a corresponding letter from "Description" in the link column)

	DESCRIPTION	LINK		TERM
1	Common nouns and purpose give rise to natural...		A	Active Listening
2	Describes interdependent reciprocities and explains how everything fits together		B	Alumni Resources
3	Time for managing expectations and to transfer ownership		C	Annotated Agenda
4	A common term for "Right-to-Left Thinking"		D	Categories
5	Seeking to understand rather than being understood		E	Deliverable
6	The _____ of _____ is to... So that...		F	Holarchy
7	The best way to capture meaning for TO-WS analysis, prioritizing hundreds of options		G	Numeric
8	The natural force behind moving from abstract to concrete		H	Preparation
9	Visualizing everything you do in advance		I	Purpose Tool
10	"You get to ride all the rides, as many times as you want."		J	Trichotomy

New leaders are concerned with humanity — they also care about people

Life is not about finding yourself; life is about _____ yourself.

Always be yourself,

unless you can be a _____.

Then always be a _____.

Hope you have a magical moment today, and every day.

Structured Note-taking

| Date: | Project: | | Page | Of |

| WHAT? | Information | SO WHAT? | Issues |

| NOW WHAT? | To Do | WOW! | Great Ideas |

Author: Participants:

Terrence Metz
Author
MG Rush Facilitation

As a Certified Structured Professional Facilitator (CSPF), lead instructor, and Managing Director of MG RUSH FACILITATION TRAINING AND COACHING©, Terrence is passionate about training students to lead meetings that produce clear and actionable results *every time!*

In addition to earning his MBA from Northwestern University's Kellogg School of Management, his professional certifications include a Six Sigma Green Belt from Motorola University, Scrum Master (CSM) from the Scrum Alliance, Certified Scrum Product Owner (CSPO), and How To Teach Online (HTTO) Certification from the Open Leadership Network, among other certifications.

Terrence's professional experience has focused on mergers, organizational design, problem-solving, process improvement, product development, and strategic planning. He also has P&L experience in highly engineered products and services (eg, Honeywell).

He has taught classes on facilitation and leadership with the Broad Institute (a research venture of Massachusetts Institute of Technology and Harvard University), Purdue University, the University of Arkansas (Sam Walton School of Business), and instructors from the Stanford University Advanced Project Management Program (who wedged in his five-day professional class between Christmas and New Year's), along with numerous private organizations and departments of local and federal governments.

His decision-making tools for galvanizing consensus, including *Perceptual Mapping* and *Quantitative TO-WS Analysis*, are used worldwide. In 2004, he introduced the concept of holism to the field of structured facilitation as a method for keeping discussions on target, aligning deliverables within and throughout an organization, and creating traction for facilitators to lead meetings that get results.

Having taught nearly 400 classes and 4,000 students, Terrence is a talented instructor, focused listener, and equally adept at both teaching the MG RUSH FACILITATION TRAINING curriculum and at facilitating consensual agreement around important and challenging issues for groups, organizations, and teams.

Bridging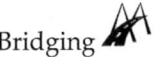

50-Minute Agenda Example

MG RUSH FACILITATION
TRAINING & COACHING
+01.630.954.5880 tel
http://www.mgrush.com/

GIRLS INC. / STRATEGIC PLANNING PREPARATION SESSION

Our meeting **PURPOSE** IS TO . . . provide mutual understanding about framing the next strategic planning session, SO THAT . . . you can orchestrate and prioritize the actions required that support your Mission and help accelerate progress towards your Vision.

SCOPE: Girls Inc. personnel, beneficiaries, and stakeholders that are targeted for your community services and social contributions over the next three years.

MEETING OBJECTIVES:
1. Familiarity and understanding with each other and the impact of the planning session
2. Agreement on strategic planning workshop purpose, scope, agenda, and simple agenda
3. Assignments about logistics and next steps

AGENDA:
I. Introduction
   Suggested Outcomes:
   - ☑ Meeting one another for the first time
   - ☑ Agreement/ modification to this meeting's purpose, scope, objectives, and agenda

II. Background Information Exchange
   Suggested Outcomes:
   - ☑ Improved understanding about the importance of a structured approach
   - ☑ Improved understanding about organizational aspirations and longer-term goals

III. DRAFT Strategic Planning Purpose, Scope, Deliverables, & Simple Agenda
   Suggested Outcomes:
   - ☑ Drafted workshop purpose, scope, simple agenda, and deliverables

IV. Logistics
   Suggested Outcomes:
   - ☑ Consensually agreed upon session timing and logistics

V. Next Steps
   Suggested Outcomes:
   - ☑ Assigned roles and responsibilities moving forward

V. Review and Wrap
   Suggested Outcomes:
   - ☑ Testing for clarity, alignment, and omissions

Meetings That Get Results — Participant's Guide©

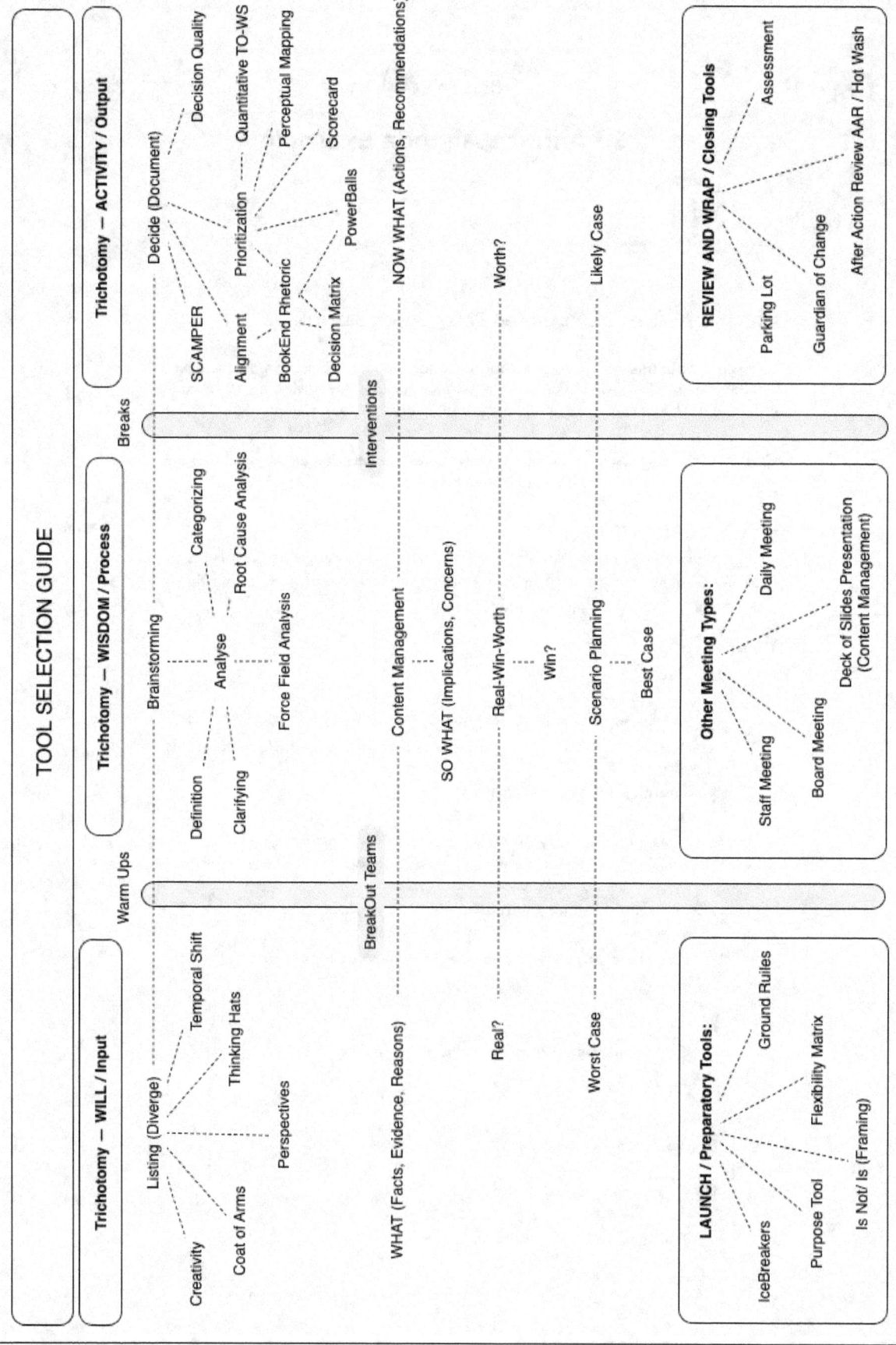

Slides & Notes

Reference Guide for Tools and Page Numbers

Flag on this page so you can refer to it quickly.

Tool	Page Number
Actions	164
After Action Review	234
Alignment	167
Analogy or Metaphor	123
Annotated Agenda	109
Board / Committee Meetings	263
Bookend Rhetoric	193
Brainstorming	132
Breakout Teams	138
Breaks	256
Categorizing	142
Clarifying Tool	185
Coat of Arms	139
Communications Plan	174
Content Management	258
Creativity	221
Decision Matrix	195
Definition	152
Flexibility Matrix	259
Force Field Analysis	223
Framing	261
Ice Breakers	97

Tool	Page Number
Intervention	260
Interviews	106
Introduction	93
Measures	148
Meeting Assessment	104
Parking Lot	102
Perceptual Mapping	202
Perspectives	226
PowerBalls	191
Purpose Tool	184
Real-Win-Worth	204
Review & Wrap	101
Roles and Responsibilities	170
Root Cause Analysis	232
SCAMPER	240
Scenarios and Ranges	242
Scorecard	196
Staff Meetings	262
Temporal Shift	147
Thinking Hats	229
TO-WS (SW-OT)	153
Warm-ups	239

Meetings That Get Results — Participant's Guide©